Hilo Rains

Hilo Rains

---

by Juliet S. Kono

Bamboo Ridge Press
1988

This is a special double issue of *Bamboo Ridge, The Hawaii Writers' Quarterly,* issues no. 37 and 38, Winter and Spring 1988, ISSN 0733-0308.

ISBN 0-910043-15-9
Library of Congress Catalog Card Number: 88-24236
Indexed in the American Humanities Index

Published by Bamboo Ridge Press.

Cover design by Susanne Yuu
Cover by: Ann Asakura Kimura
Graphics by: Leslie Chibana
Thanks also to the editors of the following publications where some of these poems first appeared: *Bamboo Ridge, Hapa, Hawaii Review, Literary Arts Hawaii, The Paper,* and *Malama i ka Honua.*

This project is supported by a grant from the National Endowment for the Arts (NEA), a Federal agency. It is also supported, in part, by a grant from the State Foundation on Culture and the Arts (SFCA). The SFCA is funded by appropriations from the Hawaii State Legislature and by grants from the NEA.

Bamboo Ridge Press
P.O. Box 61781
Honolulu, Hawaii 96839-1781

Library of Congress Cataloging-in-Publication Data

Kono, Juliet S., 1943-
Hilo rains.

(Bamboo ridge, 0733-0308 ; no. 37-38)
1. Hawaii—Poetry. 2. Plantation life—Hawaii—Poetry. I. Title.
II. Series: Bamboo ridge ; 37-38.
PS3561.0515H5 1988 811'.54 88-24236
ISBN 0-910043-15-9

10 9 8 7 6 5 4 96

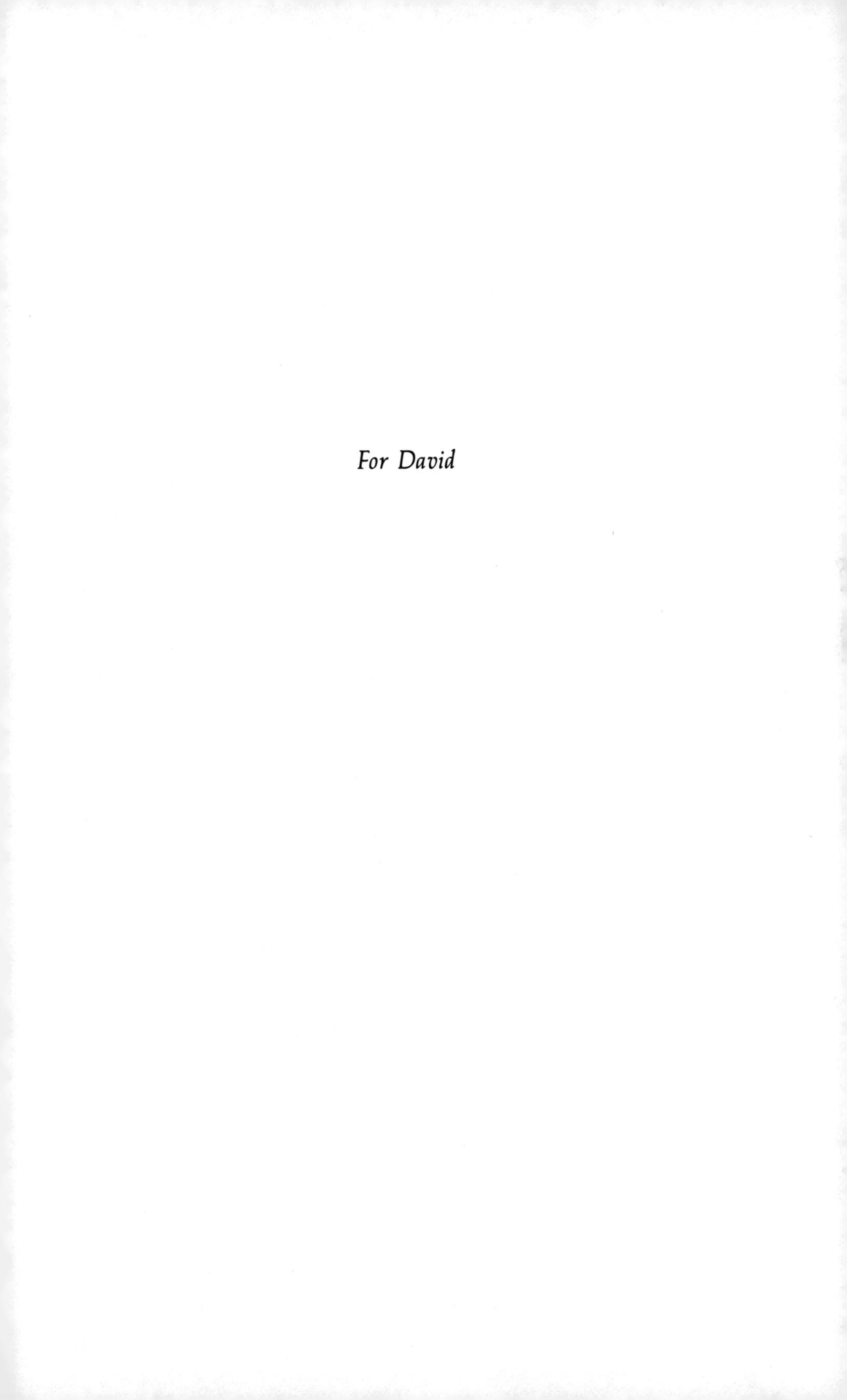

For David

I wish to acknowledge the many contributions of my parents, Yoshinori and Atsuko Asayama, my mother-in-law, Elizabeth M. Lee, and the members of the Bamboo Ridge study group.

Special thanks to my husband David Lee, Cristina Bacchilega, Leslie Chibana, Eric Chock, Mavis Hara, Gail Harada, Ann Asakura Kimura, Darrell Lum, Wing Tek Lum, and Patricia Mitiguy.

Part II

Part III

GRANDMOTHER

It is nothing more
than the glimpse
of a fleeting silhouette
of some contorted woman
against a light
that evokes memories of you.
Issei woman
standing sturdy,
feet apart,
before an ancient kerosene stove
adjusting the blue-flamed wick,
cooking the meals, or
weaving *lauhala* mats —
seated upon a *zabuton,*
feet folded back.

At night
when the *pueo* sweeps
over fields you've hoed,
scoring the acres of your life,
scattering its insignificant
moments, like field mice,
I balance over words
on a tight-wire of late light,
and become a silhouette
of a bent woman,
calling your name,
your shadow, to move into mine.

FACE

A boxcar slammed
into grandfather
and sheared off his face.
Grandfather lived. There
was no reconstructive surgery
for this plantation hand
and once-handsome man.
He lost his nose
and the smashed bones
of his cheeks sagged
and flattened his face.

There are no trains
making runs
from plantations anymore.
The closest thing
to these trains
are the restored ones
housed at the Bishop Museum.
Recently, I walked
among them and roamed
the insides of the empty cars.
I closed the door
to one of them,
placed my cheek
against the warmth
of the rough door's boards
and Grandfather's voice
resounded from the cane bulks
and backs of bent men,
vibrating my facial bones,
urging tenderly
my own face to form.

THE CANE CUTTERS

The brave Hawaiian moon
sits in the saddle of morning,
bucking its light.
A woman shivers as she trudges
briskly, behind a man. She carries
the lunches and an old kerosene lantern
that trails fumes heavily into the gloom.
Surrounding them, piles of bagasse
sit silently fat and rank.
The old-looking couple stop to rest.
The man takes out two long knives.
They sparkle in the careless light.
He fingers each honed edge
and tenderly caresses the sharpness.
Pleased, he hands one to his wife.
Together, they work the tall burnt fields,
long into the tiring hours.
They sing and they dream
to the pendulum swing of machetes.

HOE HANA WOMAN

Face and arm wraps shield her
from the sharp spiked edges
of pliant cane leaves.
Deep into the fields she moves,
mindful of the baby on her back.
She splays the rich red dirt
with flat cumbersome *tabis*
and the sun hits hard
as she swings her heavy hoe.
She levels the grass
that competes for growth
with newly-planted cane.
And in a dry reedy voice,
she sings her plaintive songs.
Occasionally, she swings
her newest child to feed
from heavy breasts
and she cries at the soft pain
of the child's bite
which is as inevitable
as her longing
for a better life.

FOR COMFORT

At sixteen,
Grandmother gave birth
to her first child.
Her dream was to take this
baby back to Hiroshima
for her aged parents
and sisters to see.
Too poor, she never went
back to wade the soothing
waters of her father's rice paddy,
or slide back
the *shoji* doors,
once open like arms.
Did she leave the
one connection,
unmailed letters—
written about this child
as evidence of her regret—
for me to find
years later, while rummaging
through the camphored chests?
Did she ever turn
for comfort
to the man who was,
by arrangement,
her husband?
Or was he too proud to gather
his young wife and child,
tenderly, like petals?
She simply
took the world on
like the child wrapped
upon her back,
walked into the fields
and let fall the light
incessant rains

upon their dark
uncovered heads.

HOME BREW

In a brown and
crude ceramic cask
he prepares rice
for the home brew—
the mixture ferments,
bubbles, and sours
like bad memories.

At night, he sips
the heated *sake*
to drown an echo of voices—
  a dead child's
  a sickly wife's—
into forgetfulness.

With eyes closed
and chin dropping onto his chest
he sings a *naniwabushi*
his body swaying like cane
in hot wind.

He strains the dregs
through layer upon layer
of burlap and rice bags,
feeding it later as fodder
to his pigs
to fatten them,
to soften their meat.

And the pigs
swing their heavy bodies
about like bells.
They grunt and snort
and bear his drunk
deadened eyes,
his flush, stagger,
and loose tongue.

GRANDMOTHER AND THE WAR

She memorizes the Pledge of Allegiance,
the Star-Spangled Banner.
Everything Japanese is buried:
her Buddha, the Rising Sun, family pictures.
She makes a garden on this mound
and all the days of war, she tends silence.
But late at night, she shakes off
the dead leaves of her reticence
and rising from the garden of her voices,
I hear her whisper,
"Sanae, Sanae, we are *Nihonjin*,
never forget that!"

BLACK-OUT BABY

The Japs, my mysterious kin,
have just bombed Pearl Harbor.
Each night thereafter, each home
is allowed one blackened light.
Windows are tarred
and cracks under doors
are stuffed with rags,
chastising the light that dares to wander.
The block wardens come,
drawn like termites to light.
Violators are startled
by the bang on the door
and if you are a Jap,
you have to be careful—
they could send you
to internment camp,
somewhere in Colorado.

One night, a woman labors in the heat
of the black-out light.
Into this darkness, a child is born.
It is I. A black-out baby—
nosing in the darkness
with heavy eyes,
a "yellow-belly,"
filled with a livid cry!

WARTIME

The door closes the day
to us at six.
Cloistered, we are mere shadows
behind the blackened and
pinned-down windows.
The houselights direct
their small, concentrated
beams in bald circles
on the table tops.
Mother has dinner
on the table by then,
and steam from the rice,
and the thin clicks of chopsticks
sever the dark silence.
Gas masks for the adults
and "bunny" masks
for the children
hang on the wall
like insects.
We go to bed early.
We learn the dance of shadows
on the ceilings,
the urgency of a curfew.
Only Mother stays up.
She writes long, unanswered letters
to interned relatives.
She reads or crochets.
Her ears become keen
in the silent music of waiting
and her eyes grow sharp
but distant. They glisten.
It has been a long time
since she's been outside
to gaze at the expanse of the heavens;
she aches for a look
at the stars and the moon.

INTERNMENT

Corralled, they are herded inland
from Santa Rosa.
After the long train ride
on the Santa Fe,
the physical exam,
the delousing with DDT,
the branding of her indignation,
she falls asleep.

Days later, she awakens
in an unfamiliar barracks—
Crystal City, Texas—
on land once a pasture.
Not wanting to,
not meaning to see beauty
in this stark landscape,
she sees, nonetheless,
through her tears
on the double row
of barbed wire fencing
which holds them in
like stolid cattle,
dewdrops,
impaled
and golden.

TSUNAMI: APRIL FOOL'S DAY, 1946

Sun-bleached houses
of Shin-machi line one end
of Hilo Bay
like crooked teeth.
Sampans creak and mar
the stillness of this
unsuspecting fishing village.
But soon sea birds take flight,
lecture their premonitions.
Groups of silence
spring to attention.

Curious, we bite
into the porch railing
with our bellies
and watch the tide recede.
Sleep-loosened hair
caresses our faces,
the morning air.
We hear a rumble far off;
something's coming in.
And before we know it,
a tsunami has us walled in.
The warnings come too late.
We children are hurriedly piggy-backed
by Aunt Miyoko and Mother.
Father rushes out
to start his Model-T.

Namu Amida Butsu.
Mother puts her hands together
in *gassho.* Water curls
above us like a tongue
lashing; it breaks apart the house.
The kitchen *tansu* crashes
with Mother's wedding china.

We lose sight of Grandmother.
We head out for the car
but we never make it.
We all link hands.
Reminded to breathe deeply,
warned to never let go,
we all go under.

The wave's force shoves us
this way and that.
Our *miki neko* drowns
clawing the last shriek
of the house. Things
sink in this widening mouth of water
foraging for the young and old,
those weak on their feet,
or in their will.
Life burdens us.
It seems easier to give up
and die. But when air bursts
into our lungs we grow hopeful.
We cling to things we can grasp.
We float with debris
and bodies whose whitened
and astonished faces
all look familiar.
We retch and gasp.

The tsunami tries three times
to gulp us into the mouth
of its watery womb.
Exhausted, finally,
the water subsides and ebbs
once more
mindful only of the moon.
The aftermath leaves people

dazed and horrified.

Flies come in hordes
to taste death.
People come to claim the bloated
bodies of relatives and friends.
Scavenger crabs run about
picking at flesh,
delighting in this new abundance,
while people collapse
in the solemn stench
of putting things to right.

THE OUTHOUSE

On radio station KIPA,
broadcasting from
The Naniloa Hotel, overlooking
the shores of Reed's Bay,
Eddie Fisher sings
"Oh My Papa"
when unduly interrupted
by a news flash.
The broadcaster says
lights flickered
in some parts of
New York City,
and the bodies
twitched for what
seemed like
massive minutes
when the switch
was pulled.
The Rosenbergs
are executed,
August, 1953.

One continent,
one ocean away,
the biggest question
at Grandpa's
Kaiwiki farm is
whether or not
he should bury the old outhouse
and install an indoor toilet.
It is dangerous
to have opinions;
one could be accused
of being Communist!
It is crucial for me
that Grandpa acquire

an indoor toilet.
I cannot go on
visiting him
at his farm,
especially if lights
in the old outhouse
flicker each time
kona winds blow.

AN AFTERNOON

Steam rises from the cast-iron
kettle and burnt *kiawe* coals tinkle
like the flow of *a'a*.
Once in a while, I spread coals
with a guava branch
and duck the acrid blue smoke.
Grandpa goes to the chicken house
and with a wire crook,
hooks at a chicken's leg,
pulls the squawking chicken forward
and with twine,
ties its leg securely to a tree.
He does this a dozen or so times.

Grandpa slits the chickens' throats
with a deft flick of his wrist
and a sharp bolo knife
that makes blood spurt
into a retaining bowl.
The blood will be cooked later.
I squat and watch from
the perimeter at this rite,
and smell the warm blood-tendrils
unbraid the chickens' lives.
And even as
parts of the chicken twitch,
they are dipped whole
into the hot kettle of water,
and Grandmother, my aunts, and Mother
pluck swiftly at the feathers.
White feathers fly
to the matted circle of ground.
The feathers are hot
and Mother grabs at her ear lobes
to cool her fingers.

The featherless chickens
are then strung from
the navel orange tree to cool,
and from the far side,
the excited poi dog noisily strains
on its rope, hoping to steal one.

Some of the chickens will be sold.
Some are stored and one or two
are roasted to a furious brown
in the old dutch oven.
Everyone is ravenous by dinner time.
Hot gravy is poured over rice
and served with chicken
I cannot stomach.

RICE BAG SHEETS AND PILLOW CASES

Before polyesters, the drip-drys
and the permanent presses,
over a hot kerosene stove
Saturday mornings,
Mother made starch
that bubbled its thickness
like hot-springs mud.
Into a long, white porcelain bathtub,
she laid out sheets and pillow cases
made from sewn-together rice bags.
The faded calligraphy on the cloth
meandered
in the shallow tub of water
in purple displacement.

My sister and I pulled
and wrung the warmed sheets
like *mochi,* then hung them dripping
on the clothesline, to dry.

By late afternoon, the sheets
were stiff and they flapped
like wayward sails caught in the
blustery trades as we gathered them
in accordian folds
before the evening dampness set in.

Late at night, while in bed,
I'd turn my face into the warmth
of the freshly starched sheets
and rub my face and legs along
the fine sandpapery surface
that crinkled like ricepaper,
and I would breathe in deeply,
the fresh smell of earth and grass,
the hot yellow sun,

and from it gathered
the rich warm scent,
suggestive of mothers and grandmothers
drifting remotely in passive
but unfaltering assurance
in the sweet warm fibers
of that day's poor cloth.

HILO RAINS

The house has
no paint on its walls.
Wind whistles through
cracks of
mismatched planks.

There is no ceiling.
I look up
to the underside
of a rusted iron roof
supported by

rough-cut beams.
From the porch,
I look down
a sloping canefield
into which

the family men
disappear daily
until dusk. Beyond
the fields stands
Wainaku Sugar Mill;

and beyond that,
tiny Waiakea Village,
deep-set,
facing Hilo Bay.
I sit for

hours staring:
through trees
toward the henhouse
where on its roof
on sunny days

Grandma places
heavy *futons* to air,
while high-wheeling
Hawaiian hawks
look down

for stray hens;
at the Otas' house,
surrounded by
wild peach trees,
two enormous

rain tanks
and old, rusted plows,
fingers gaffing the air.
Toward evening,
we women wait

with sewing
on our open laps,
for the parting
of cane to occur
within the fields.

It would announce
men back
from work.
But often,
the weather is bad.

Winds send
rains cascading
sideways across the land,
rippling cane tassels,
dropping nearly-

ripened fruit,
sending in the warm
odor of manure,
of burnt sugar cane,
and the slow fog,

while we keep watch,
swinging our lanterns,
yellow beacons
to guide home
the tired cane-men.

EGGS

With arms crooked around
unraveling loops
of our egg baskets,
we walk
to the chicken coops
in single file
like Buddhist nuns;
I, chaste as a novice.

Grandmother places
the newly-laid eggs
into the baskets
where they wobble
on the bottom
of these wicker nests—
eggs I pick up and press
against my breasts
to feel their warmth
spread over me like hands.

We carry the eggs
into the kitchen,
sort them out on trays:
    white from brown
    small, medium, large.
I help candle them
for neighborhood marketing.
Bloodspot-tainted ones
I isolate
like menstruating women
    in old tribal custom.

I marvel at those eggs
ovaled to perfection.
Holding them up to the light,
my clumsy hand shimmies

the opaque albumen
    like some distant sea
    I dream of
under its fragile shell.

And the suspended yolks
are like my unborn children,
that I would someday,
far away from this light,
break
from their salty fluids.

MENOPAUSE BABY

Woman of no recourse,
she hopes Nature
stands on her side
the last years
of formal womanhood,
but it is cruel even now.
At forty-eight,
she conceives another child.

There is no mistaking
the signs. In their green
wholesomeness, *napa* cabbages
in her garden turn up
their cloned heads to mock her
double chin, sagging breasts
and flattened buttocks.

Exhausted of motherhood,
she goes about the camp
inquiring "ways."
Other women refer her
to people who may consider it.
Prices she cannot afford to pay.
This leads her
to rely on
old wives' tales:
the golden ring
or burdock root,
riding a horse,
binding the navel,
drinking pomegranate juice.

Afraid for this child,
she lets it stay.

GOOD-BYE TO OLD WAYS

The grocery vendor
from Kawamoto General Store
blows his horn
and Grandma, Grandpa, and I
spill like rice from the house,
shuffle into the unsurfaced road,
crunch the loose lava cinders
like rice crackers,
thinking of things to buy.

The vendor greets us with a bow,
and opens his truck
of smelly imported goods.
Not tempted, Grandma goes
down her list carefully selecting
only things she needs:
Hatada bread, *soda-mizu,* grape jelly,
candles and incense for the altar,
and some rock candy for me.
I stare from under Dutch-cut
bangs nearly covering my eyes.

The vendor talks story with Grandpa.
Grandma pays the bill.
The vendor bows again
when accepting the money,
then figures change on his *soroban.*
After securing his truck,
the vendor bows again
as if in apology
or gratitude—one cannot tell.

Grandpa walks ahead.
Grandma follows
carrying the packages.
"*Opa* me, Grandpa, *opa* me."

I beg to be carried.

So he squats,
swings me on his shoulders,
and seats me on top of our world.
I turn to wave
at the vendor's truck
writhing in the dust,
then to Grandma,
her old ways,
good-bye.

SULFUR

Women gathered
like chrysanthemum bouquets,
talked quietly among themselves.
These mourners,
in hushed voices, talked idly
of who married whom,
the new babies,
the sicknesses, other deaths.
I overheard them whisper
that the fifty-pound bags
of yellow-white granules—
delivered to your house
and banked like logs
against the outhouse,
used in bleaching
the green pandanus leaves
to whiteness in deep redwood vats
for the weaving of hats,
mats, and purses,
for tourists in Waikiki—
caused your cancer.
Working the sulfurous fumes
day in and day out
was suspect.

And I remember
the day you died.
Grandmother, in her anger,
dragged the left-over sulfur bags
to the top of the hill
and shook them furiously,
to the wind—
much as I imagine
she must have done,
in different fervor,
lifting her skirts
up for you.

THE WAKE

I'm in the lead car.
Uncle drives—
our headlights on,
a small purple flag
on the car's hood
marked "Funeral"
flutters in the wind.
Behind us, a slow hearse
carrying Grandfather's body,
and back of it,
a long line of cars.
The procession
files past Wainaku Camp.
Then, after the fork,
we turn right,
head up Kaiwiki Road.
Along the way,
the curious
and friends
come out of their houses
to the roadside
to watch. Some salute
or cross themselves,
others place hands
over their hearts.

Later,
a Buddhist Wake
in the dark parlor
of his plantation house—
I see Grandfather's
"old-time" plantation boss,
some Filipino friends
straight from the fields,
others in old zoot suits,
and the Puerto Rican,

we only know as "Bu-zing,"
who makes his home
by the river,
in a bamboo grove.
The Japanese women
help serve the meatless *okazu,*
and the men
receive donations
of rice and money,
record the *koden*
in composition tablets.

The Portuguese have come too:
the young girls in white,
like Madonnas,
smelling of sweet bread
baked that morning;
the men in riding boots,
sadness tucked
under their moustaches;
the older women in a group,
black mantillas
looped over their heads.
One, a spokeswoman says,
"Ah Mama-saan.
We so sorrry.
Your Paapa,
he *make* too youung."
Grandmother bows.
She dabs her eyes
with one hand,
and with the other
she takes the women's
outstretched hands.

The *Bonsan* intones his *okkyo.*

blessing the gray and open coffin
banked by sprays of white orchids.
Family members go up,
one by one,
to the make-shift altar
in front of the body,
and offer incense
pulverized like human ashes.
I drowse in the long service
and listen to a strange
blend of sounds:
the *okkyo,*
the click of rosary and *juzu* beads,
and the Portuguese women softly chanting
"Ave Maria gracia plena . . ."
commending Grandfather's body
to Christ.

THREE USES OF CHOPSTICKS

I.

She drops her head between her knees.
Her long black hair flows over.
She gathers the strands,
flips up her head
and twists her hair
into a silken bun.
She takes a pair of chopsticks,
sticks them into her hair
to hold it up; together with an orchid,
chopsticks make a practical decoration.
The nape of her neck is exposed
tempting him to touch it.
At the right moment tonight
she will pull out the chopsticks
like a knife
and drop her hair
for the kill.

II.

Teeth-chipped red lacquer chopsticks
with wood exposed like flesh.
She saves the old ones for him.
He uses the chopsticks to prop
orchid plants heavy with flowers.
From her window, she watches
him stab into the cinder
at the base of the plants.
He is careful of the aerial roots—
blue-green veins more familiar now
than veins on her breasts
that he once tracked
after parting her long, graying hair

fallen across her chest.
She notices he binds chopsticks
and stalks with soft wire
in an unlikely embrace,
preventing winds from toppling
and crushing the plants.

III.

She walks down the path
like a bride — white orchids
fluttering like butterflies in her hands —
to where he waits for her.
She loops white hair
straggling from her bun
over an ear as she walks.
Fronting the small stoop
near gas burners, she bows,
draws a pair of long steel chopsticks
from their case. She picks up
the char-free bones
left among the ashes:
fragments of hip bones, pieces of skull,
parts of teeth.
She drops them into an urn.
She then ties a black cloth
around the copper box,
sticks flowers into the square knot,
and folds her arms around him
and orchids.

OJICHAN

"Now don't you girls go bothering *Ojichan*—you hear? *Ojichan* needs plenty of rest."

"What's he got, Mom?" I asked.

"He has *gan*—in the liver."

"What is *gan*?"

"Cancer, Sanae, cancer."

"So dat's what the 'horse doctor' tol' you," my father, skeptical of all doctors, said to my mother who had just returned after taking Grandfather to Hilo Hospital for some X-rays.

Mother then relayed Grandfather's poor prognosis to the rest of the family. The adults decided to hide Grandfather's condition from him. They also cautioned us, his grandchildren, from saying anything to him. We scattered like chicks whenever he approached and we hid under our mothers' wings of concern.

Grandfather turned formidable, strange, and distant. The smell of cancer, of death, followed him everywhere and lingered in the air. His skin became gray like the coating of ash on *kiawe* coals, and loose masses hung like the family dog's jowls on his once robust arms and face. The aunts, especially, fussed over him to no end.

"Papa, you want something to eat?" or "*Otosan*, you want to go *obenjo* . . . toilet?" or "Here, let me turn on the radio for you—got Japanese program right now." On and on they went, hovering over him. Congregating in groups of two or three, the adults spoke in hushed voices and the children became extremely polite.

One day, Grandfather cornered my mother, the oldest of his children, in hopes of talking to her about his condition.

"*Atsuko, anno ne, moshika* . . ." he started to say hesitating. "Listen to me, just in case . . ."

"Papa, don't talk like that, okay?" she said, cutting him off—he understanding the English better than he spoke it.

"*Atsuko, yukoto wo kiite kudasai. Kore wa, moshika dake,*" he said trying again. "Just listen to me. This is only just in case."

"Everything's going to be all right, Papa. By the time the *kibi* ready to cut, you going be all better, so don't worry, okay?"

"*Demo* . . ." he protested. "But . . ."

"*Mo-o, ijanaika,*" she insisted. "Enough, already. Don't worry." Following Mother's example, no one listened to Grandfather; everyone dismissed his anxieties.

My grandparents lived in Kaiwiki, above Hilo town, on several acres in a small house and land leased from the Wainaku Sugar Plantation. There, on the Hamakua coast, my grandparents grew sugar cane and wove *lauhala* mats be-between cane harvests. But now Grandfather was unable to do much. One Sunday, when the whole family had gathered there to help with work in the fields, to feed the chickens, and tend the garden, and when everyone seemed preoccupied with some chore or other, I happened to be on the porch, perched on the railing, hugging a post, and watching the *koi* in the pond below when Grandfather came ambling out of his room. He sat on the rocking chair on the porch and basked in the afternoon sun in what seemed a brief respite from pain. He noticed me as I moved to steal away.

"*Oiii, Sanae, yokattana,*" he said upon noticing me. "Good. Come-u, come-u ova hea." He gestured widely with his hand and thwacked his boney thighs for me to sit on.

"Nahhh, I better not. Mom's gonna scold me—she like you rest. Anyway, I too big for that."

"Come-u, come-u. *Ojichan* like-y on-e talk-u to you."

"Okaaay," I said, hopping down from the railing, looking to see if Mother was anywhere around. Grandfather and I sat quietly together and we rocked in his chair. We had done this frequently before his illness.

"Sanae . . ." he started to say at one point.

"You want something?" I asked nervously. I was afraid he would ask me something about his illness and how was I supposed to answer? But he didn't answer me and drifted back into thought.

"*Ojichan*," I then said, "tell me one story, like before time."

"*Mmmm, so-o dayo*," he nodded. "Good idea. Wat get, guru kine story, eh?"

"Oh, any kine story you know, okay."

"You *pololei, anno, Urashima Taro?*"

"Yeah, I think so—but I forget already. I learn that long time before—at Japanese school."

"*Yoroshi*," he said. "Good. *Mukashi, mukashi, sanzen-nen,* get all-same guru boy, *Urashima Taro,* wen save-u *anno* tetaru, no? from one all-same no-guru boy-san. *Wakaru ka*?" he asked, "You sabe?"

"I think so. Long time ago, had one good boy, *Urashima Taro,* who wen save one turtle from one bad boy, right?"

"*So-o so*," he said, nodding his head as he proceeded with his story. "An' tetaru, all-same very, very, hap-pi. Give-u boy-san allu-kine presento."

"But . . ." I protested. Grandfather continued.

"Den one time, *Urashima Taro* go hishing, no? And all-same big-u tsunami come-u and wash-y *Urashima Taro* fa'away."

"But *Ojichan,* that not like the story," I said.

"Tetaru den come-u save-u *Urashima Taro.* Dey swim-u long-u time. Jes' like-y *anno tori, ne*?" he said suddenly, pointing to a flock of birds banking over the cane.

"What you talking, *'jichan.* Dey wen turn into birds—'s what you said? Dey magic or what?"

"Ehhh, magic-u tetaru take-y *Urashima Taro* way insasai da wata. Long-u time dey stay insai da wata. Den *Urashima Taro,* him live-u long-u, long-u time. Him get long-u life. *So-o ne,* very long-u, long-u life," he said with a sigh and a far look in his eyes.

"You get the story all wrong, *Ojichan*."

"Ha, ha, ha, ha. *Ojichan* make-y story all-u *kapakahi,* no? Sanae, *Ojichan* tell you *kāpulu-kine* story."

"'s okay. But they lived happily ever after, right?"

"So-o dayo. Kokoro no naka ni," he said. "In the heart."

"Wha . . .?"

Just then Mother started calling me. "Sanae, Sanae, where are you?" Coming out of the house, she saw me sitting with Grandfather. She bustled over. "I told you before," she said, shaking her finger, "you are not supposed to bother *Ojichan.*"

"I know. But I wasn't bothering him."

"Now don't you answer back."

"But mom, he was just telling me a story."

"Don't 'but' me, young lady," Mother said in an even louder voice. Having lived on the Mainland for many years, she sounded all the more *haolefied* and clipped the angrier she got. "Now go outside and play with Brian folks," she said.

"But . . . I hate play with Brian dem. They play dumb kine games.

"Sanae," Grandfather then whispered to me. "Bum-bye Ojichan tell you notha story. Mo bettah you go . . . no? *Yoisho,"* he groaned, sliding me off his lap.

Having heard all the commotion, others in the family came out to the porch and milled like animals around a fire —including Brian who said, "Troublemaker. You always like cause trouble—you know that?"

"So, I don't care."

"What you wen tell *Ojichan,* anyway?"

"None of your business. Go 'way, okay? Jes' leave me alone," I said.

"You think you so, so smart," he said, sticking his pink lizard tongue at me.

Meanwhile, Mother and my aunts went about clucking and fluttering about Grandfather, checking to see if I had spilled any of the birdseeds. Satisfied that I had not said anything to Grandfather about his illness, Mother steered him back to his room. Because everyone felt I was the most hapless and apt to say something to Grandfather, I was reminded, again, not to go near him. I complied. But as the days fell off the weeks, how I craved to sit on his lap again; how I wanted him to tell me a good story. But Grandfather was inaccessible as the navel oranges on the topmost and thin branches which hung temptingly on the trees in his backyard. Ones we left to rot.

I'm quite certain Grandfather knew, all along, about his poor health. Sometimes, from behind the thin walls of his plantation, I could hear his lament. He wanted some kind of confirmation of his condition. Depending on his state, he also desired to go back to Japan for a visit.

"*Bimbo shite, kuro shite,—konna no mono ni natte*... I was so poor and I faced so much hardship—and to end up like this..." he said to Grandmother, hoping for some kind of reaction to his statement. And later "*Mama, mo-o ichido—Nihon e kairitai, naa*... I wish I could go back to Japan—one last time..."

With this knowledge, the family started making the necessary travel arrangements. But just as suddenly, Grandfather stopped nagging about going back to Japan. Soon after, his condition worsened dramatically. Our family, missed all the cues to help him with his reality. In our own denial, we kept on speaking about Grandfather's upcoming trip—the one he was going to take when he got well. How he must have laughed at us. Even then, Grandmother persisted in not telling him he was going to die.

"*Watashi was shinitonai, demo*..." I heard him say one day. "I don't want to die, but..."

"*Dame dayo, sonna hanashi,*" Grandmother scolded. "It is foolish to speak that way." She dismissed Grandfather's entreaties with some other matter. "*Kyo wa ii otenki da na-a, ne Papa?* Today is such a lovely day, isn't it?"

As time passed Grandfather grew more and more withdrawn and from behind his eyes, I saw nothing but resentment. Once our eyes met. "*Ojichan,*" I said from across the room, wanting to go up to him. His eyes answered me with the roundness and the sadness of a turtle's. He shook his head at me when I ventured forward.

"Mo betta you listen yo mama. Bum-bye Mama toe-o much-y *huhu,*" he said stiffly as I watched his eyes take flight.

Spring passed by with the snap of a finger. Even if school finally let out in June, I was not happy about facing all those summer days stretched out like a rolling sea. Melancholy lapped my days. During that time, my parents, sister, and I lived in Hilo Town. My grandparents left their home in Kaiwiki to live with us in our tiny two bedroom duplex apartment on Kilauea Avenue. There, Grandfather lived out the last days of his life. My grandmother wanted to be close to the hospital despite the fact that the doctor had told her nothing further could be done.

To do our part, my sister and I gave up our bedroom to our grandparents and we slept in the parlor on thin *futons* on the cold, linoleum floor. My mother took leave from her Territorial custodial job to help Grandmother care for Grandfather. Mother learned how to administer injections and her job was to give Grandfather his often begged-for morphine shots. Toward the end, however, Mother cheated and gave Grandfather shots on demand rather than at prescribed times.

"Atsuko, Atsuko, chusha wo . . . hayaku," Grandfather called out one day. "Hurry, give me a shot . . ."

"Matte ne, Papa?" Mother answered. "In a minute, okay?" She hurriedly prepared the syringe. Firmly grabbing Grandfather's leathery arm, Mother inserted the needle.

"Ughhh," she exclaimed, horrified when the needle bent after its insertion into Grandfather's thin and shriveled arm. "Why didn't it go right in?" Mother questioned struggling to get the needle out, beads of perspiration foaming above her lips. *"Chotto ne, Papa? Gomen,"* Mother said. Turning to me, she said, "Go get the pliers—the one in Daddy's fishing box." "One moment, okay? Sorry about this."

"Hayaku, hayaku," Grandfather mumbled. "Hurry, hurry."

His lower lip trembled as the pain dragged knives through his body. Once Mother got the opiate in, Grandfather relaxed his arched body and Mother swabbed his bloody arm. Before falling asleep, Grandfather grabbed Mother's arm and looking at both of us he slurred and said, "'*tsuko, Sana . . . nakuna yo.* Don't cry."

Grandfather's death made an ordinary day vividly memorable. I remember the colors — the dark green leaves of the *hāpu'u* lining the yard, the gray of the overcast skies, the red flowers on the hibiscus bush; I remember the sounds — the high whine of flies, the low murmur of voices, the throb of the chanting; I remember the odors — the delicate smell of flowers and the pungent one of incense. Most of all I remember feeling the warmth recede from Grandfather's hands and feet, and the chill of the white, rice-bag sheets.

We had just finished eating lunch. I slipped outside before Mother could stop me and I joined the yellow jackets droning monotonously in the hot, humid air. It drizzled lightly, off and on. Perspiration-soaked tendrils of hair stuck to the nape of my neck like caterpillars. The mock orange hedge circling our house exuded, as if from a gangrenous wound, a sweet funereal scent into the oppressive, humid air. I fastened my skates and skated the sidewalk fronting our house, moving my arms like a swimmer trying to drown everything out. I skated my heart out. Up and down, up and down the block I went. I jumped compulsively over the lines, over the cracks in the walk.

"Step on a crack, break your mother's back. Step on a crack, break your mother's back . . ."

Perspiration burned my eyes. The skate key tied around my neck on a grocery string banged incessantly on my flat chest with every jump I took. I was obsessive in my energy. Periodically, I keyed my Oxfords tighter into the skate stays and took up my ritual again. "Step on a crack, break your mother's back," I chanted.

Over and above the scratch and drag, I managed to hear

Mother calling me. Her voice was frantic.

"Sanaeee. Sanaeee," she called.

"Whaaat?" I yelled back. "I'm over heeeere."

"Go get Fuji Sensei. *Hayooo* . . . hurry. And don't dilly-dally."

"But Mom."

"Go on. Go! Go!" She clapped and shooed me away with a backward wave of her hands.

I didn't want to fetch the priest. I wanted to go back to the house. I knew Grandfather was dying. I wanted to be with him. But I obeyed my mother. I went for the priest.

The Honpa Hongwanji Mission, the Buddhist church I attended every Sunday and the place where the priest resided, was situated only a block away. But the high temple with its bell tower seemed to recede as I skated toward it. I skated with all my might. I swung my arms and caved my body in for speed. "Sanae, Sanae," I heard my grandfather calling. I imagined myself on the back of *Urashima Taro's* turtle transporting me deeper and deeper into the depths of the high-towered, pot-bellied building where the priest sat meditating in front of the Buddha.

"Hurry. Please hurry. My mother wants you at the house. My *Ojichan* . . . he's dying." I didn't wait for an answer. I bounded back on my turtle and swam the concrete sea home.

Mother was waiting for me at the top of the stairs when I arrived. I kicked off my skates and leaped the steps in twos.

"Where's the priest?" Mother asked.

"He's coming!" I waved my arms as I tried to catch my breath. "*Ojichan*, he's . . .?" Mother nodded her head. I started to cry. "You knew I didn't want to go. You knew I wanted to be here—and you still made me go." I was furious at my mother for sending me out.

"I know," she said, "I know."

"Ah huhhh! If you knew, then why? Why?"

Mother said nothing more. She let me rave. She later led me into Grandfather's room where my father, grandmother, sister, and an aunt stood by. I fell to the side of the bed. How I wanted to be there at his side to watch him die. Oh, how I wanted to watch what I thought would be the most morbid but truly loving thing in my life. How could you, I thought to myself. How come you couldn't wait for me—how could you go ahead and die without me here?

We drove the body back to Kaiwiki and all the relatives assembled at Grandfather's house. Not wanting to offend any of our ancestors, the family carefully followed all the Buddhist traditions. At the wake, Grandfather was given a Buddhist name—and he was no longer Bunyemon Oshita, immigrant, and American alien, but from then on he was referred to by his Buddhist name: *Koshin,* Happy Faith.

So where are you, *Ojichan*—*Koshin*? At sea, riding the turtle, perhaps? Or are you in this air, somewhere, flying as a bird?

The days before the funeral, Buddhist chants, perfume from the flowers and incense smoke filled the air. Bored with it all, some of my cousins took out Grandfather's old B-B gun—the mongoose gun—to shoot at cans stuck on the fence post.

"Don't shoot at anything moving," Brian teased, looking my way. "It might be *Ojichan*."

"Shut-up," I said. "He was my *Ojichan* and he'll come back as something good. You'll see. Maybe a bird so beautiful you wouldn't believe it. Not like you."

"You're so weird," he said. "*'jichan's* pet. *'jichan's* pet." He teased with a touch of envy.

Not long after the funeral, my parents, sister, and I went to Kaiwiki to visit Grandmother. There, I walked alone into the quiet of Grandfather's tall and swaying cane. Thinking about his death, I searched for solace in his fields. I broke a branch from a guava tree nearby and with the long stick, I swung hard into the cane. Wham. Wham. I whacked the stalks and startled the nesting birds with each violent swing. *Ko-shin. Oji-chan. Ko-shin.* Suddenly, the cane turned into a swaying green sea. The rice birds flew up and swirled around like fish. And I was riding *Urashima Taro's* turtle once more—driving deeper and deeper into the green. Looking up, I waved at each bird flying by. I waved good-bye frantically. *"Ojichan,"* I called out. *"Ojiiichaaan."*

Asayama photo collection

II

SMOKE

Grandmother strikes
a match
and lights her lantern.
She pushes
the light and smoke
ahead of her.
She enters your room
and taps the soles
of your feet.
You must get up soon,
cut cane with your father.
She then shuffles
to the kitchen
where she strikes
another match
to the kerosene stove.
The light bites the wick,
billows a dark web.
Its odor permeates the air.
She adjusts the fire.
Flames of blue teeth dance
behind the small mica window
as she starts breakfast.
Later, she serves
the Buddha and your father
the day's first bowls
of rice.

You are thirteen.
Your father has made you
quit school. You can
no longer play
with other girls.
You must now cut cane
like a man. And everyday
you watch the *lunas* burn

adjacent fields
where yellow flames crackle
and lick high into smoke
filling your coughs.
Soot rains. The skies
look overcast as if someone
has tossed a throw-net
over you and hauled you in—
a good day's catch
for the next day's work,
and the next.

Late afternoon,
you look toward the house.
A toothpick-thin plume
rises from the *furo* stack.
Someone has started the bath fire.
By the time you get home,
the bath will be ready,
but it receives
your father's body first.
Later, you peel clothes
off cane scratches, blisters,
and insect bites welting
a torso beginning to curve.
The hot water soothes you,
burns your open sores.
Blood pulsates in your ear.
You emerge from the water
with body steaming
as after a passing shower
suddenly hits a hot
open field. *Furo* smoke
clings to your *yukata*,
your hair.

After dinner,
you and your father
sit on the porch
to watch the night.
You roll a cigarette,
light it for him.
He permits you drags—
the source of a long addiction.
You blow smoke
into the hazy distance
and flick ashes
into an empty sardine can.
You take turns
on his cigarette—
the only acknowledgment
he makes of you,
his cane-cutting daughter
who works like a man
but cries silently
like a woman.
And he never bothers to look
at you. He stares straight ahead
into the night,
blowing smoke
fragile as lace
from his nostrils.

THIS YOUNG MOTHER

As proof of migrant success
this picture was taken
to be sent to Kumamoto-ken.
No one smiles in this formal portrait.

Everyone looks proper for the occasion:
Grandmother sits in the center, hands on her lap.
No one can see the scars on her hands
she wrings like a dish towel.
My *nisei* father stands to Grandmother's right
having given his mother the seat,
a Japanese male's rightful position.
Father is American; proud of the difference.
Standing in front of Father,
my older sister leans on the chair.
My sister appears curious but anxious.
Mother stands to the left of everyone.
I'm in her arms. My right hand
is extended and pointing toward the camera.
I'm barely one but already trying
to touch what's not there.
Mother looks prim, steadfastness
flowing over her bodice like the broad
white choirboy collar she wears.
She doesn't yet know
all the sorrows she will face—
some of her children will die,
another run away.

Recently my mother explained why
this photograph was never sent,
or framed on the wall,
or placed on the coffee table
like the rest of the family photographs,
but hidden in a *tansu* drawer.

This young mother didn't know
her slip was showing.

AFTERMATH: APRIL 1, 1946

A tsunami
generated by an earthquake,
epicenter the Aleutian Islands,
destroys Shin-machi,
the tiny fishing village
where we live,
to one side of Hilo Bay.

A cracked sea wall,
warped sheets of the iron roof,
water-tossed lumber
and a smashed Model T Ford
form the rubble,
our home.
Flies swarm everywhere.

Mother retrieves from the sea muck
odd pieces of her china,
crocheted doilies, tablecloths,
embroidered pillow cases—
items of a hope chest.
Clothing and underwear hang
like rags, flags of distress
on the collapsed house,
disaster knowing no modesty.

Mother cries over her oil-stained
wedding kimonos, photographs,
the rich silk obis—
sashes tying her
to her sentiments.

And for days she stands
before a wooden wash board
with a bar of Castile soap
in up-to-the-elbow hot steamy water.

She scrubs and cries.
Once in a while,
she gasps
as she chokes down a sea
that keeps rising in her.

COUPONS

My sister and I
were put to bed
early in the evening;
restless
upon scratchy tatami mats
spread on the floors,
our small bodies
tucked to chin
under thick comforters.
And Mother stole away
as soon as our eyes flickered
like altar candles.

She slipped into the kitchen to clip coupons.
And we tossed to the
high, thin snips
of her dressmaker's scissors
as they echoed back
into our Spartan room.
The venetian blinds
were drawn on Kilauea Ave.
The shaded 40-watt bulb
swung its poverty
over the newspaper-
and magazine-littered
table where she sat.

She made long lists
and tangled herself
in grocery tapes,
dropped loose change
and the years into
empty mayonnaise jars.

Today, she dresses
in the same conservative

grays and blues.
Her hair is twisted
into a tight-fisted bun
and she wears
square, rimless
Ben Franklin glasses.
She never spends
with wild abandon,
although she has the means
and is no longer constrained
by the needs of a family.
And she still clips coupons—
content to redeem
small bargains in her life.

SONLESS

To our sonless dad,
we were daughters,
substitute sons.
We dressed in blue-jeans,
braided our hair,
and concealed it
under baseball caps.
To please,
we often followed Dad,
an avid off-shore fisherman
from Shin-machi,
who, his eyes
sternly shanked to the sea,
baited the long, lean hooks
more tenderly
than he held his daughters.
This man,
whose blend of two worlds
made for cruel longings—
"*Otosan*, Dad,"
the name to use
we never knew.

To our sonless mother,
we were daughters
who helped fill a void,
the failure of the womb.
We were urged to catch
the pitches Father threw at us
and while our soft, feminine hands
may have smarted,
we never let on.
And on Sundays,
we watched
the team's star pitcher,
cheered him on.
After the games,

we listened
to men talk story,
eat pupus and drink
their Lucky Lagers.

Meanwhile, Mother
of constant faith
went to the Hongwanji Mission
to pray to Buddha.
What prayers did she pray for us?
That all opportunity
be bestowed on us
like men we cheered and followed?

Sisters, "sons" of the same water
we treaded long.
The fathoms of childhood
now shrouded in black,
lie in an old shoe-box
like the dead birds we buried,
popsicle sticks bound
as crosses. In the boxes
lie the laughter, the crying,
the yearning of young girls
growing up. Whatever sons
in the running
were soon out-distanced.

Now Dad no longer fishes
and is too old for baseball.
He golfs instead.
Occasionally, we
join him. We are
friends in our strange
mixture of heritage.
We have suffered
our differences.

MEMORIAL DAY

You bring along
a shoyu gallon of water,
dendrobium flower sprays
cut from your garden,
and a totem of tangerines
held in place
by a sharpened chopstick
thrust through their centers.

You do *haka-mairi* yearly
as a promise kept
to your mother and father
to be guardian of this grave
the years would have forsaken.
You are the eldest,
held responsible.

You place the fruits and flowers
before a lichen-covered headstone
then light candles and incense
chanting
the *Nembutsu*
under your breath.

With tears in your eyes
you tell me the story:
how your mother
fed this child its death
with milk
that grew rotten in her breasts;
how this baby cried for days
before it died;
how your father carried your mother
upon his back
to go to the grave site;
how your older sister's body

was washed, dressed, and transported
to this burial place
by mule cart.

You pour the gallon of water
over the headstone.
Gurgling water
spills over the years,
the element-muted name.
"To wash the stone," you say,
"to give my thirsty sister a drink."

PEARLS

I hung my face like a moon
over the galvanized kitchen sink
to watch Mother clean
the *aholehole* Father caught
while pole-fishing off Suisan,
a sampan dock,
in Waiakea Village.
She scaled the fish
with a spoon, a scale
or two
spiralling into the air
like snowflakes.

She slit the silver bellies
like a surgeon—her fingers,
shriveled like dates,
disappearing into the cavities.
In one pull,
she had the gills
and guts out, intact.
Looking my way,
she shook her head
at my scale-flecked face
as she washed each fish out.

The luminous fish
made a neat row
on the cutting board.
They were then salted,
dredged in flour,
and pan-fried in oil.
She tried to teach me
how to eat these fish.
I watched her work
her chopsticks
picking bones clean

of whitened meat.
I watched and tried to imitate.

I will
never acquire the knack
of eating fish,
especially the fish head,
the way she eats it—
having no qualms about
sucking out the brains
or the gelatinous eyes
with a slurp
and plopping from her mouth
into a cupped hand,
the eyeballs,
like pearls.

FOURTH OF JULY

With each of us at an elbow,
Mom and I maneuver my father
like a small boat,
his thin body weathered by age
and a series of strokes.
We ease him backwards
into a chair on a lanai
at the Hilo Hawaiian Hotel
where we have been invited
to watch the fireworks
lofted over Coconut Island.

Born early in the century,
my father headed full sail
into the wind—
faced the Depression, the wars,
his thirty-year mortgage,
and his impertinent daughters,
with a hardheadedness
all his own,
sailing, finally,
into the calm waters
of a comfortable
but short-lived retirement.

I wish more fire in him
like what bursts up front,
but he is moored to passivity
like the buoy marking the shoal.
As I watch him look up,
I see that his mouth
is wide open
consuming the dark.
Up ahead, the trades blow
the firefall out
toward the breakwater.

And my father
is caught
in the failing light
like the sailboat—
its sails shaking down,
its spars laid bare
as it fades
into the starless night.

OGO PICKER

At twilight,
above the ocean's din,
I hear the peal
of the cowbell
that hangs
from Father's fishing pole.
I hear him calling.
His voice is storybook golden,
like the sunset.
He's calling me
to see the silver *papio*
he has caught while casting.
But the wind
scatters the direction
of his voice,
distends the sound.
His words hollow and gong out
a litany of ancestral names:
Shige, Bunyemon, Tori, Gisaburo.
Dying has the stamina
of temple bells.
I cannot find him.

In the distance,
in a tide pool,
Mother is knee-deep in water.
Habitually thrifty,
she wears a *lauhala* hat,
a white halter top,
madras Bermudas—
cast-offs from her daughters.
She is oblivious
to the clouds and mountains
in the water with her
as she picks *pipipi* and *ogo*
off dark, volcanic rocks.

I seek her to tell her
that I cannot find my father.
I want her to comfort me
but she has me
locked in my room again.
She is stringent
with her affections.
Her breath smells
of iodine, salt and little love.
We do not cry together
our salt tears.
She is the way she is—
old-fashionedly cold
and unsympathetic—
what her upbringing dictated.
I do not reproach her.
"It was to survive,"
she once said.

I leave her there
reflected in water,
embracing it.

RECONCILIATION

Mother,
we hold on to
opposite ends
of this old oilcloth
which has outlasted my childhood.
We snap it apart.
Together, we swing the cloth
over the kitchen table
and smooth over the familiar folds.
We touch.

You place items
from the center of your life
onto one end of the table:
horse-hair brushes,
a jar of water,
sumi ink, whetstones,
and rolls of rice paper
to practice calligraphy
and *sumi-e* drawings.
Skills taken up
after retirement
to affirm the past.

Black brush strokes
slash the white expanse.

Your passion
shames me.
Ancient scrolls
unroll from your fingers:
pine trees, their moon,
birds in grasses,
lines of *tanka*
or *haiku*.

What discipline
you bring to your art—
something you felt
you could never instill in me,
your upstart and wayward
American daughter.

Minutes pass.
You straighten
and hold up your drawing
with fingers fastened
to the paper like the clothespins
of past laundry chores
I failed to do when asked.
Ashamed of being different
and poor,
I would answer back
by disappearing
to town or a movie
at the Hilo Theatre
rather than help you.
The scoldings later
fumed like the smell
of Clorox bleach
surrounding you:
"You have no discipline,"
you'd say.

I look over your shoulder
at the still life you've captured.
You're forgiving
of the small imperfections
you find in your drawings
as you have long forgiven
those found in me.

Mother, I have a confession.
I, too, have long forgiven you
for never having finished school
beyond the eighth grade,
for speaking with an "island" accent,
for us being poor,
and Japs.

Finished, you place your brushes,
these extensions of your fingers,
these obliging children,
into the Welch's jelly jar
of clear water,
and you and I watch
the black ink swirl,
float out.

Asayama photo collection

SASHIMI

You call
eating sashimi
primitive.

I slice pieces
from a slab
of my favorite fish,
abura shibi,
from Kekaulike Market.
Upon a blue plate,
on a bed of shredded *daikon*
and *chiso* leaves,
I fashion
thin, red slivers
of raw fish
into a pinwheel.
In the center
of this wheel,
I place a dollop
of *wasabi* mustard,
into a flower cup
cut from a carrot.

I dissolve
the pungent mustard
into the shoyu sauce,
the aroma exciting
my ancestors—
they dance
on my tongue.
I pierce
a slice of fish
with my chopstick,
dip it into
the sauce.
I close my eyes.

I let the smooth fish
slide over my teeth,
my tongue,
then swim down
my gullet.
I chase this fish
with a mouthful
of hot rice,
some green tea,
and smack my lips
in ancient noises
of satisfaction.

I take another piece.
Looking up,
I toast you
with this trembling
delicacy.
Soon you will come
to appreciate
the years
behind my palate.
And I am patient
as all love is patient,
for you will learn
as you once learned
with women—
to close your eyes
and take
flesh
to mouth.

OBON FESTIVAL

For Clarence

I. The Ritual: Bon Dance

Kimono-clad dancers
circle a song tower
in slow deliberate rhythm:
hands clap, drums boom,
cut deep into the sternum.
Reed flutes and singers whine.
Hands clap once more.
Voices banter back and forth
in unison
at appropriate motions,
moments.

Slow flailing hands pick up speed,
progress to increasing frenzy.
The inner circles go faster,
then faster.
The dancers shout,
"Betcho, betcho, kusare betcho!"
They curse that
which gives birth to us.

I join the inner circles.
I dance for the dead.

II. Aftermath: Tsunami, 1960

Rings of bodies
sway in and out.
They move like waves.
If you look up into the sky
while dancing,
you can tangle yourself
into the net of stars,

lose yourself,
enter the dance.

I've done this before.
This time I dance for you—
celebrate your death.
I clap my hands,
dance all summer long,
list in sadness.
I move in circles.
I search for brave centers.

But the power of the sea
is overwhelming.
It pulls me out.
I move and sway like stars caught
in reflections
of slow curling waves.

III. Toro Nagashi (The Boat Ceremony)

Candlelight shows your spirit the way.

A hundred Japanese lanterns
help light the path.
The miniature boats move out.
My eyes feel the weight
of the arched bridge
spanning the wide mouth
of the placid Waialoa.

The Buddhist priest in dark robes
blesses with chants and bells
each boat headed out.
All carry candlelight beacons
on their shaky wooden bows

to guide those
lost or drowned.

Tiny lights float toward darkness,
to where the still river waters drain,
become brackish and cold;
to where the chop of the river meeting sea
rocks the boats.

IV. Survivor

Summers never end here.
This was your season.

The fuchsias still hang in
abundance over the gate.
Gardenia and camellias
suffocate the stillness of the air
with their sweet, funereal scents.
The air is warm,
stifling to those
who live and suffer.

These days,
I keep on dancing,
learn new moves:
ways to clap my hands,
to light candles and *senko,*
and I still find
sufficient need
to move with the stars.

AMATEUR PHOTOGRAPHERS

The air is serrated
by the sea-birds' cries.
They come in on the wind.

Below us, sea kelp
dance loosely
in wide shifting currents.

Surgeon crabs on the Point
scatter at the sound
of our approaching feet.

Colorful sea-shells
devoid of life
litter the break-front.

The low sun that sparkles
on the water, follows
the curve of your body

like a sadness, as
we move toward
the water's edge

in search of perfect light.

IN THE LIGHT OF YOUR BONES

To David

The white-bellied *'akekeke*
are the first to walk
the early morning beach.

They leave three-slotted
prints, helter-skelter on the sand.
Crabs lift their antennae,

sidle down to the sea.
In this hour, you are already
embracing Kōnāhua-nui's first light.

The light and quiet enfold you.
I'm listening to honking cars
and the day's noises as they

rise to a steady crescendo;
you are climbing deeper
into solitude. I wait for you.

Evening comes and I watch
for your light. You descend
from the mountain,

like a singular star,
moving toward me,
holding fires of tranquility,

tender silences burning in you.
And I wait patiently
to curl in the light of your bones.

SILVERSWORDS

At cold daybreak
we wind
up the mountainside
to Haleakala Crater.
Our hands knot
under the rough of
your old army blanket.

We pass protea
and carnation farms
in Kula,
drive through
desolate rockfields.

Upon this one place
on Earth,
from the ancient
lava rivers,
silverswords rise,
startled
into starbursts
by the sun.
Like love, sometimes,
they die
at their first
and rare flowering.

CAR SOUNDS

Some very late nights
after much drinking,
Uncle Roy's car sounded
loud in the hush of
the cold country air.
This aroused an icy
anger in Grandfather
that sizzled like steam
on the car's hot tail-pipes.

It was easy to learn
their comings and goings—
knowing whose
car sounds they were:
Uncle Roy's Plymouth
had an efficient sound,
with its smooth and deep
wind-up into third gear
on that last stretch before home.
Then it geared down
before entering the cool cave
of the narrow, *totan* garage.
Aunt Sue's second-hand Dodge
was her first car.
She drove in on weekends
from her secretarial job
in Naalehu, Ka'u.
Her car ran quietly.
But she gassed it when
she arrived home,
in order,
I always thought,
to announce her arrival.
Upon her departure
Sunday afternoons,
children and dogs ran

after her in a funnel
of red unsettling dust.

For years after that,
when we moved to Hilo Town,
it was Mother's car
up the driveway
or Father's noisy truck
at five o'clock, after work.
And Mom and Dad in turn
got to know the rhythm and rail
of their own standards,
when late at night
they'd wait and listen
for the cars to pull up
into the driveway,
when we daughters
first learned to drive.

And I'm like a child once more—
on the bend of a driveway,
in a white, by day's end,
dirtied pinafore—
as I wait for you.

I know
you would never leave
to never come back,
and as you drive up,
your old car does sound
as if it had crossed the
old wooden bridges above the flumes,
traversed the deep-rutted
dirt canefield roads,
swept through the deep muttering
of the long

and God-forsaken rains.

You're driving home those
sounds of yesterday with you—
their timbre,
the dissonance,
the impatience.
You're chugging home
in fits and starts,
but love,
so dependably!

SURFER

It is late.
You are sleeping
in the other room,
the television still on,
your blue
blanket tousled
like surf breaking
in the Pacific Ocean.
And your body is the image of
the wind-burnt one
confronting the murmuring
winds at Walo's;
cupped hands shade
your eyes
as you watch for the sets.

Your great-grandfather,
Bunyemon,
the one with the difficult
samurai name
you often mispronounce
in the language
you protest learning,
sailed at seventeen
to come here.
He crossed the same
ocean that mesmerizes you.
You are the same age he was then.
And if
he were to sail in today
to meet you here,
he would hardly recognize
you—your face melted
down by the sun,
featureless compared to his,
craggy with wants.

Lamenting, he would have
questioned his bearings.

You take a deep, long
breath as I'm writing this.
Your chest shudders
with the wrap
of sleep's relief.
Outside, the tacky
sands whip and the
sticky waters lap
persistently against
our house.

I cannot take away
your loneliness,
as I must struggle with mine.
I drive you down to
Point Panic instead,
pretending to take
you there to see if
the surf's up.
But I take you there
to watch your eyes.

At the beginning of the ocean,
I can push you into
a part of the Earth's kiln,
to glaze the gentleness of blue,
fire quiescence,
burn the sea into you.

YONSEI

I hear the music
ride the updraft
in this valley.
It is not yours.
You are thumbing
your way to the North Shore:
being dropped off
at Left Overs
or Thompson's Corner, first,
before making your way down;
shouldering a radio,
smothering the speaker
into your ear—
the one with the gold star
that glints and steals
studs of moonlight
when your hair whips
away from your face.
I can see the wide
swagger of your body
as it moves.
Shadows of firm bones.
They hold your body
across roads as each
lean and tall muscle
ripples you forward
in your dark, good health—
each sinew curved,
warm as sun.

You live so far
from what connects you.
You have no recollection
of old plantation towns,
of rains that plummeted
like the sheaves of cane,

the song of flumes,
the stink of rotting feet,
the indignities of hard labor.
Your blood runs free
from the redness of soil.
But your *zoris*
are caked with mud,
your dreams mixed in sun,
wild surf, and turbulent air.
And yet once a year
you come with me
in your dark brooding—
like a craving—
to visit the ancestors'
gravesites to pray.
You say nothing
about being held
to these traditions.
You pray, bow and
burn incense. You travel
backward in time
for a brief moment
and say dutiful words,
do the respectful gestures
and I know that
in my longest sleep
you would come
and I would not want.

Photo by DBL.

Juliet Sanae Kono Lee was born in Hilo, Hawaii in 1943. She grew up there during the last years of the Territory before moving to Honolulu. After raising her children, she returned to the University of Hawaii where she is currently studying for her B.A. in English.

She has published her poetry in *Bamboo Ridge, Hapa, Hawaii Review, Literary Arts Hawaii, The Paper, Malama i ka Honua* and other publications.